W9-BMZ-026

FAMILY WORSHIP

In the Bible, in History & in Your Home

DONALD S. WHITNEY

Family Worship: In the Bible, in History, and in Your Home

The Center for Biblical Spirituality, Shepherdsville, KY 40165

Published 2006
Printed in the United States of America on acid-free paper
15 14 13 12 11 10 09 08 07 06   2 3 4 5 6

ISBN 10: 0-9785238-0-6
ISBN-13: 978-0-9785238-0-0

The author wishes to thank Jared Hallel for his design and layout work, and Vickie Cochran and Jeff Robinson for their editorial help.

For information regarding additional copies of *Family Worship* and other publications, see www.BiblicalSpirituality.org or write:

The Center for Biblical Spirituality
379 Pine Creek Road
Shepherdsville, KY 40165 USA
Info@BiblicalSpirituality.org

Whitney, Donald S.
    Family worship: in the Bible, in history, and in your home / Donald S. Whitney
    iv, 64 p. ; 22 cm.
    ISBN 10: 0-9785238-0-6
    ISBN-13: 978-0-9785238-0-0
    1. Family—Religious life. 2. Christian life.
    BV200.W45   2006
    249.W612f

TABLE OF CONTENTS

For my family—past, present, and future
and
For my spiritual family in Christ—local and universal

INTRODUCTION

Some time ago, I was in England and heard a report on BBC radio about a government study there indicating that, as a result of TV, technology, and the like, families rarely spend time together. The study observed that conversation between family members has "degenerated into an indistinguishable series of monosyllabic grunts." And what was the recommended solution to this dilemma? The government should teach a series of classes instructing families how to talk and play together.

I have at least two responses to this report. First, things are really bad when the government believes that the family is in trouble. Second, God has a much better plan for family time together than classes taught by the government.

I had gone to England to speak at a conference. Around the table there one evening, I heard the story of a minister's family who had not acted as though God has a better plan until it was too late. The minister's widow told me that the greatest regret of her life was that her late husband had not begun leading their family in daily worship together until after he had been diagnosed with terminal cancer.

Contrast that with a story sent to me by a friend describing what he and his four siblings said at their parents' fiftieth wedding anniversary celebration. He wrote,

All five of us children decided to express thanks to our father and mother for one thing without consulting each other. Remarkably, all five of us thanked our mother for her prayers and all five of us thanked our father for his leadership of . . . family worship. My brother said, "Dad, the oldest memory I have is of tears streaming over your face as you taught us from *Pilgrim's Progress* on Sunday evenings how the Holy Spirit leads believers. [When I was only] three, God used you in family worship to convict me that Christianity was real. No matter how far I went astray in later years, I could never seriously question the reality of Christianity and I want to thank you for that."[1]

The latest figures I have seen from the North American Mission Board of the Southern Baptist Convention report that 88% of churched youth in the US leave the church once they finish high school.[2] Researcher George Barna's statistics are only slightly better: "When [churchgoing teenagers were] asked to estimate the likelihood that they will continue to participate in church life once they are living on their own, levels dip precipitously, to

---

[1] Joel Beeke, *Family Worship* (Grand Rapids, Mich.: Reformation Heritage Books, 2002), 3.
[2] As reported by Alvin L. Reid, "Raising the Bar: Ministry to Students in the New Millennium." Available from http://www.alvinreid.com/raisingthebar.html, accessed 19 October 2005.

only about one out of every three teens"[3] saying they expect to stay in church.

One of the problems with these numbers is, unlike the siblings at the fiftieth wedding anniversary celebration, most of these young people have no lifelong, sweet memories of family worship. If they had them, such memories might prevent their departure from the faith in the first place. Or if they do walk away, the memories might be the means to return them to the faith later.

The great British Baptist preacher of the 1800's, Charles Spurgeon, spoke to this issue, saying,

> Brethren, I wish it were more common, I wish it were universal, with all [Christians] to have family prayer. We sometimes hear of children of Christian parents who do not grow up in the fear of God, and we are asked how it is that they turn out so badly. In many, very many cases, I fear there is such a neglect of family worship that it's not probable that the children are at all impressed by any piety supposed to be possessed by their parents.[4]

[3] From a January 10, 2000 article at www.barna.org, "Teenagers Embrace Religion but Are Not Excited About Christianity," accessed 11 January 2000.
[4] C. H. Spurgeon, "A Pastoral Visit," *Metropolitan Tabernacle Pulpit*, vol. 54, (London: Passmore and Alabaster, 1908; reprint, Pasadena, Tex.: Pilgrim Publications, 1978), 362-363.

I am persuaded that so little family worship regularly exists in Christian homes, that even in *most* of our *best* churches, *most* of our *best* men do not lead their wives—and children if they have them—in family worship. Another recent survey by George Barna supports that claim. According to his research,

> Eighty-five percent of parents with children under age 13 believe they have primary responsibility for teaching their children about religious beliefs and spiritual matters. However, a majority of parents don't spend any time during a typical week discussing religious matters or studying religious materials with their children. . . . Parents generally rely upon their church to do all of the religious training their children will receive.[5]

Having your family in a good, Bible-teaching local church is crucial to Christian parenting. But this is not enough for conveying to your children all you want to teach them about God and your beliefs. Moreover, it is unlikely that exposure to the church once or twice a week will impress your children enough with the greatness and glory of God that they will want to pursue Him once they leave home.

---

[5] Barna Research Group, May 6, 2003, as quoted in *Current Thoughts and Trends*, July 2003 (vol. 19, no. 7), 21.

This is why family worship is so important. But even more importantly, God *deserves* to be worshiped daily in our homes by our families.

Chapter 1

"As for me and my house, we will serve the Lord."
Family Worship in the Bible

The Bible clearly implies that God deserves to be worshiped daily in our homes by our families. There is no direct, explicit commandment in Scripture about family worship. The practice of it, however, is implicit throughout the Bible. To quote Spurgeon again,

> I trust there are none here present, who profess to be followers of Christ who do not also practice prayer in their families. We may have no positive commandment for it, but we believe that it is so much in accord with the genius and spirit of the gospel, and that it is so commended by the example of the saints, that the neglect thereof is a strange inconsistency.[6]

Evidence for the practice exists as far back as Genesis 18:17-19. This is where the Lord and two angels have appeared to Abraham in the form of dusty travelers. Abraham provides hospitality for them, and in the course of the

---

[6] C. H. Spurgeon, "Restraining Prayer," *Metropolitan Tabernacle Pulpit,* vol. 51, (London: Passmore and Alabaster, 1905; reprint, Pasadena, Tex.: Pilgrim Publications, 1978), 327.

conversation it begins to dawn upon Abraham who his guests are, especially when one of them says that Sarah will soon find herself expecting the child that the Lord promised to the old, barren couple years before. As the three are leaving and heading toward Sodom and Gomorrah—which the Lord is about to destroy—the Lord speaks:

Shall I hide from Abraham what I am about to do, since Abraham will surely become a great and mighty nation, and in him all the nations of the earth will be blessed? For I have chosen him, **so that he may command his children and his household after him to keep the way of the Lord** by doing righteousness and justice, so that the Lord may bring upon Abraham what He has spoken about him.

We have no reason to believe that much true worship of the true God existed in Abraham's day. In fact, after the Tower of Babel episode in Genesis 11 in which the Lord confuses the languages of people and scatters them, it would be difficult to identify anyone in the Bible who loved God. But as He did centuries earlier with Noah, God graciously chose Abraham and revealed Himself to him. And He did so in part, we are told, "so that he may command his children and his household after him to keep the way of the Lord." When would Abraham have done this? He did not have others to rely upon. He could not turn for help to the ministries of a local church. The only way Abraham could have commanded his children to keep the way of the Lord was to teach the things of God at home.

Once Abraham and Sarah's miracle baby, Isaac, arrived, it is obvious that Abraham did more than merely provide a good home education in times of formal and informal instruction about keeping the way of the Lord. Abraham obviously led Isaac and the rest of his family in the worship of God. This is plainly implied in the story of Abraham and Isaac in Genesis 22. God tested Abraham by telling him to offer up Isaac as a sacrifice. Early the next morning, Abraham obeyed by getting everything together—even splitting the wood himself—and heading for Mt. Moriah. There he intended to sacrifice his only son to God because of his faith in God, and his confidence that God would raise Isaac from the dead.

Those familiar with the story will know that the Lord intervened at the last moment and provided a ram to be sacrificed as a substitute for Isaac. But in Genesis 22:6-7, Abraham did not yet know that Lord would intervene and spare him the agony of killing Isaac. Isaac knew they were going to the mountain to offer a sacrifice and to worship God, but he did not yet know that the plan was for him to be the sacrifice. Abraham and Isaac had traveled for two days and were at the foot of Mt. Moriah. As they prepared for the final leg of their journey, we read that

Abraham took the wood of the burnt offering and laid it on Isaac his son, and he took in his hand the fire and the knife. So the two of them walked on together. Isaac spoke to Abraham his father and said, "My father!" And he said, "Here I am, my son." And he said, "Behold, the fire and the wood, but where is the lamb for the burnt offering?"

How did Isaac know that they did not have everything necessary for a sacrifice? How did he know that the worship of God involved fire, and wood, and a lamb, and that the lamb would be sacrificed as a burnt offering? It is because he had long been familiar with sacrifices and the worship of God. Isaac had often seen the wood split and piled for a sacrifice. He had heard the crackle of the fire and smelled the burning flesh of a lamb offered to God. Isaac knew when an element of the worship of God was missing because Abraham had frequently led his family in the worship of God.

Perhaps the best-known text in the Bible commanding families to teach their children is Deuteronomy 6:4-7:

Hear, O Israel! The Lord is our God, the Lord is one!

You shall love the Lord your God with all your heart and with all your soul and with all your might. These words, which I am commanding you today, shall be on your heart. You shall teach them diligently to your sons and shall talk of them when you sit in your house and when you walk by the way and when you lie down and when you rise up.

There is much more here than family worship. Family worship would comprise only a part of obedience to this command, but it would be a part. Parents should teach the things of God to their children at every opportunity, and they should do so with the children individually and collectively. But both in biblical times and now, the best time for parents to teach the things of God to their children on a *consistent* basis when *all* the children are present would be in a time of family worship.

Have you ever considered how infrequently people gathered for congregational worship in the centuries comprising the entire Old Testament? Even after the tabernacle and temple were built, groups of believers did not gather together to worship God as often as is sometimes assumed. Only after the Babylonian exile, late in Old Testament history and hundreds of years after Solomon built the temple, did the local synagogues develop and people begin to worship God congregationally on a weekly basis. Of course, with the coming of Jesus and the anointing of the Holy Spirit upon all God's people since Pentecost, believers are now privileged to experience the riches of being in God's family through regular participation in a local church.

But God was as worthy of worship in the days before regular congregational worship as He is now. True believers in God, such as Abraham, Isaac, Jacob, Joseph, Moses, Joshua, and others wanted to worship Him in their day as much as His people do now. Keep that in mind as you read the famous words of Joshua 24. This great successor of Moses had led them into the Promised Land and been the leader of God's people for decades. Near the end of his life, he once more exhorted the Israelites to remain faithful to God. In Joshua 24:15 he declared,

If it is disagreeable in your sight to serve the Lord, choose for yourselves today whom you will serve: whether the gods which your fathers served which were beyond the River, or the gods of the Amorites in whose land you are living; but as for me and my house, we will serve the Lord.

How would Joshua and his house have served the Lord? Part of serving the Lord for them then, just as it is for us now, is worshiping the Lord. But in a day when congregational worship was so infrequent—after all, it usually involved a trip of several days to travel to the tabernacle—regular family worship would have been a part of how Joshua carried through with his resolve, "as for me and my house, we will serve the Lord."

In Psalm 78:1-8 we read the inspired words of a psalmist named Asaph. He was one of the three leaders of music appointed by King David in the days of the tabernacle. Asaph wrote,

Listen, O my people, to my instruction;
Incline your ears to the words of my mouth.
I will open my mouth in a parable;
I will utter dark sayings of old,
Which we have heard and known,
And our fathers have told us.
We will not conceal them from their children,
But tell to the generation to come the praises
of the Lord,
And His strength and His wondrous works
that He has done.
For He established a testimony in Jacob
And appointed a law in Israel,
Which **He commanded our fathers**

That they should teach them to their children,

That the generation to come might know,

    even the children yet to be born,

That they may arise and tell them to their children,

That they should put their confidence in God

And not forget the works of God,

But keep His commandments,

And not be like their fathers,

A stubborn and rebellious generation,

A generation that did not prepare its heart

And whose spirit was not faithful to God.

When would these fathers have taught these things to their children? Fathers teaching their children "the praises of the Lord," as verse four commands, is something they would have done in the worship of the Lord. Would they have taught them these things in congregational worship? In part, perhaps they would. But this passage seems to be speaking more on an intimate and family level than a congregational one. Besides, as has already been noted, even by the time the Psalms were written there was much less congregational worship than we sometimes imagine, and some of this might have involved segregating the fathers from the rest of the family. And even if the family members were all together, they were not inside the tabernacle. The tabernacle was smaller than most church buildings today, so it was a physical impossibility for all the people to be inside it. When all the people did gather to worship God congregationally—such as at one of the major feasts—everything happened as they stood outdoors together by the thousands. So the instruction Asaph spoke of almost certainly did not occur in a congregational setting; rather, fathers taught these things to their children at home. And some of that teaching happened as the fathers led their families in the most regular kind of worship they experienced, family worship.

Over in the New Testament, we read these familiar words in Ephesians 6:4: "Fathers, do not provoke your children to anger, but bring them up in the discipline and instruction of the Lord." You do not expect others to do this for you, do you fathers? Of course not. It is a command given as your direct responsibility. So I ask you, when do you do this? Yes, you do it when you bring your children to church. Yes, you do it when you converse with them about the things of God from time to time. Yes, you even do it some by example. But bringing children up in the discipline and instruction of the Lord is not accomplished unintentionally and incidentally. Yes, it should and will happen throughout the day at unplanned, serendipitous occasions, but it should also happen purposefully. Without some regularity and structure and purpose, it is one of those things that we assume we are doing but never actually do. Consistent, father-led family worship is one of the best, steadiest, and most easily measurable ways to bring up children in the Lord's discipline and instruction.

Did you know that a proven commitment to family worship is implied as one of the qualifications for being an elder (that is, a pastor)? The apostle Paul writes about these qualifications in 1 Timothy 3. In verses 4-5 he says this about an elder: "He must be one who manages his own household well, keeping his children under control with all dignity (but if a man does not know how to manage his own household, how will he take care of the church of God?)." In light of this, it is fair to ask, "If a man cannot manage worship in his own household, how can he manage worship in the church? If he cannot lead family worship, how can he lead church worship?"

In 1 Peter 3:7, the apostle Peter assumes not only that church elders would practice family worship, but that all Christian husbands would do so: "You husbands in the same way, live with your wives in an understanding way, as with someone weaker, since she is a woman; and show her honor as a fellow heir of the grace of life, so that your prayers will not be hindered." Have you realized that the prayers here are those prayed together by husbands and wives? It is also true that the individual prayers of the husband will be hindered if he does not live with his wife in an understanding way and if he does not show honor to her. But here the text speaks of mutual prayer. Peter assumes that Christian couples pray together. He expected Christian husbands to conduct family worship. This is the norm for holy husbanding. Spurgeon said on this verse, "[This] text would be most appropriately used to stimulate Christians to diligence in family prayer. . . . I esteem it so highly that no language of mine can adequately express my sense of its value."[7]

The Bible clearly implies that God deserves to be worshiped daily in our homes by our families. The beloved Bible commentator Matthew Henry knew this when he said, "The way of family worship is a good old way, no new thing, but the ancient usage of the saints."[8]

That is true not only of the saints (this is, the believers) in the Bible, but it has also been true of God's people ever since. This leads us to chapter two.

[7] C. H. Spurgeon, "Hindrances to Prayer," *Metropolitan Tabernacle Pulpit*, vol. 20, (London: Passmore and Alabaster, 1874; reprint, Pasadena, Tex.: Pilgrim Publications, 1981), 506.
[8] Matthew Henry, *Matthew Henry's Concise Commentary* (Gen. 12:6), (Oak Harbor, Wash.: Logos Research Systems, 1997).

CHAPTER 2

"HERE THE REFORMATION MUST BEGIN"
FAMILY WORSHIP IN CHURCH HISTORY

The lives of our Christian heroes testify that God deserves to be worshiped daily in our homes by our families. For instance, we know that the first generations of Christians consistently worshiped God as families. Lyman Coleman, a scholar of early church history, writes about the family worship practices of the Christians in the decades and centuries immediately after New Testament times:

> At an early hour in the morning the family was assembled and a portion of Scripture was read from the Old Testament, which was followed by a hymn and a prayer, in which thanks were offered up to the Almighty for preserving them during the silent watches of the night, and for His goodness in permitting them to meet in health of body and soundness of mind; and, at the same time, His grace was implored to defend them amid the dangers and temptations of the day, —to make them faithful to every duty, and enable them, in all respects, to walk worthy of their Christian vocation. . . . In the evening, before retiring to rest, the family again assembled, the same form of worship was observed as in the morning, with this

difference, that the service was considerably protracted beyond the period which could be conveniently allotted to it in the commencement of the day.[9]

Moving forward in history, consider the example of the heroic reformer of the church in the sixteenth century, Martin Luther. He preached almost every day, pastored a church, and wrote massive amounts of theology and Bible commentary. But Luther also recognized that like any other husband and father, he had the responsibility to be the worship-leading pastor of his family. In one place he wrote of

Abraham [who] had in his tent a house of God and a church, just as today any godly and pious head of a household instructs his children . . . in godliness. Therefore such a house is actually a school and church, and the head of the household is a bishop and priest in his house.[10]

A century later, both the Presbyterians and the Baptists considered family worship so important that they included statements about it in their confessions of faith. In the most

---

[9] Lyman Coleman, *The Antiquities of the Christian Church* (Andover and New York: Gould, Newman & Saxton, 1841), 376-377.

[10] Martin Luther, *Luther's Works,* ed. Jaroslav Pelikan, "Lectures on Genesis: Chapters 21-25" (Saint Louis, Mo.: Concordia, 1964), 384.

influential Presbyterian doctrinal statement ever—the Westminster Confession of Faith—and the most influential Baptist confession of faith ever—the Second London Confession of 1689—documents still adopted by thousands of churches around the world, the practice of family worship is explicitly prescribed. In both documents, we read this: "God is to be worshipped everywhere in spirit and in truth; *as in private families daily*, and in secret each one by himself."[11]

In fact, the Presbyterian-dominated Westminster Assembly thought family worship so important that in August, 1647 (the same year they published the Westminster Confession) they produced an entire publication devoted exclusively to this subject, *The Directory for Family Worship*. This guide contains fourteen divisions, including sections on the reason for family worship, the proper use of Scripture in it, the responsibility of the husband/father to lead family worship, directions for family prayer, and more.

But the directory was not just a collection of suggestions for the exceptionally devoted men in the church. In the preamble, the church elders were required to keep the heads of the households accountable to their God-given responsibility for family worship. If they failed, they were to be admonished privately. And for any husband or father who continued to neglect his spiritual responsibility to his family, *The*

---

[11] Section 21.6 in the LCF of 1689; 22.6 in the WCF; italics added.

Directory for Family Worship gave these instructions:

> He is to be gravely and sadly reproved by the session
> [that is, the elders]; after which reproof, if he be found
> still to neglect Family-worship, let him be, for his obsti-
> nacy in such an offence, suspended and debarred from
> the Lord's supper, as being justly esteemed unworthy to
> communicate therein, till he amend.[12]

In other words, these Christian leaders from across Great
Britain and the thousands of British churches that adopted
this document thought family worship so essential for spiritual health and so indispensable for the souls of their children, that any man who dared abandon his family spiritually
in this way was to receive church discipline.

In his classic work, *The Worship of the English Puritans*,
Horton Davies writes of "the high esteem in which Family
Worship was held by the Puritans."[13] He notes, for example,
that Richard "Baxter [1615-1691] gives a large place to the
duties of Family Worship in his Christian Directory. There
[Baxter] maintains that . . . Not only Scripture, but reason
and experience point to the necessity for family worship."[14]

---

[12] *The Directory for Family Worship* (annotated ed.; Greenville, S.C.: Greenville Presbyterian Theological Seminary, 1994), 2.

[13] Horton Davies, *The Worship of the English Puritans* (Morgan, Penn.: Soli
Deo Gloria, 1997), 278.

[14] Davies, 279.

"Then," Davies paraphrases Baxter's directions for family worship, "after supper, the head of the family is requested to examine the children and the servants on what they have been taught during the day. Then the religious duties of the day conclude with family prayers and praises." Baxter, now quoted by Davies, concludes his directions with this plea:

And now I appeal to Reason, Conscience, and Experience whether this employment [of family worship] be not more suitable to the principles, ends and hopes of a Christian, than idleness, or vain talk, or cards, or dice, or dancing, or ale-house haunting, or worldly business or discourse? . . . Persons coming into such a family, with a serious tincture of mind, might well cry out, "This is none other than the house of God, this is the gate of Heaven."[15]

A man born fifty years after Baxter, but who became just as well known to the church around the world for his commentary on the Bible, is Matthew Henry (1662-1714). His biographer wrote,

Matthew's conduct in his family, . . . was in a great measure regulated by the example of his pious father, of whose house those who had access to it were ready to say,

---

[15] Davies, 280-281.

This is no other than the house of God, and the gate of heaven. Matthew was constant in the worship of God in his family, morning and evening, which nothing was suffered to prevent. . . . He was never tedious, but always full and comprehensive, performing much in a little time, which seldom exceeded half an hour. . . . When the whole was ended, his children came to him for his blessing, which he gave with solemnity and affection.[16]

Matthew Henry himself wrote,

If therefore our houses be houses of the Lord, we shall for that reason love home, reckoning our daily devotion the sweetest of our daily delights; and our family-worship the most valuable of our family-comforts. . . . A church in the house will be a good legacy, nay, it will be a good inheritance, to be left to your children after you.[17]

And it was Matthew Henry who made one of the most remarkable of all statements on this subject. Regarding family worship he said, "Here the reformation must begin."[18]

---

[16] "Memoirs of Matthew Henry, As Written by a Contemporary: S. Palmer," in *Matthew Henry's Commentary on the Whole Bible*, vol. 1 (Old Tappan, N.J.: Revell, n.d.), vii.

[17] *The Complete Works of the Rev. Matthew Henry,* vol. 1 (Grand Rapids, Mich.: Baker Book House, 1979), 260-261.

[18] Henry, 260.

The great Jonathan Edwards (1703-1758) is known for his intellectual power and his devotional passion, his preaching, and writing. But we should also remember him for the Christian family life that he and Sarah modeled, and for the influence this had on their eleven remarkable children. Edwards, according to biographer George Marsden,

> began the day with private prayers followed by family prayers, by candlelight in winter.[19] . . . Care for his children's souls was, of course, his preeminent concern. In morning devotions he quizzed them on Scripture with questions appropriate to their ages.[20] . . . Each meal was accompanied by household devotions, and at the end of each day Sarah joined him in his study for prayers.[21]

Samuel Davies (1724-1761), the man who succeeded Jonathan Edwards as president of Princeton and described by no less than Martyn Lloyd-Jones as one of America's greatest preachers, said of family worship:

> If you love your children; if you would bring down the blessing of heaven upon your families: if you would

---

[19] George M. Marsden, *Jonathan Edwards: A Life* (New Haven, Conn.: Yale University Press, 2003), 133.
[20] Marsden, 321.
[21] Marsden, 133.

have your children make their houses the receptacles of religion when they set up in life for themselves; if you would have religion survive in this place, and be conveyed from age to age; if you would deliver your own souls—I beseech, I entreat, I charge you to begin and continue the worship of God in your families from this day to the close of your lives. . . . Consider family religion not merely as a duty imposed by authority, but as your greatest privilege granted by divine grace."[22]

J. W. Alexander (1804-1859) was a godly and influential Presbyterian minister in New York in the first half of the nineteenth century. His book, *Thoughts on Family Worship*, is the best treatment on the subject I have read. In the preface, he is astonished that "There are many heads of families, communicants in our churches, and, according to a scarcely credible report, some ruling elders and deacons who maintain no stated daily service of God in their dwellings."[23] In the brief chapters of his book, pastor Alexander deals tenderly, winsomely, and practically with subjects like "The Influence of Family Worship on Individual Piety . . . on Parents . . . [and] on Children." He writes about "Family Worship as a

[22] "The Necessity and Excellence of Family Religion." *Sermons of the Reverend Samuel Davies*, vol. 2. (Morgan, Penn.: Soli Deo Gloria, n.d.), 86.
[23] J. W. Alexander, *Thoughts on Family Worship* (1847; reprint ed., Morgan, Penn.: Soli Deo Gloria, 1998), v.

Means of Intellectual Improvement," especially in learning the Bible. He writes persuasively about "The Influence of Family Worship on Domestic Harmony and Love . . . on a Household in Affliction . . . on Visitors, Guests, and Neighbors . . . [and] on Perpetuating Sound Doctrine." I think he is most compelling when addressing the "The Influence of Family Worship on the Church" and "The Influence of Family Worship on Posterity." But in his concluding chapter he says bluntly, "Laying aside all flattering words, I may say plainly that I regard the neglect of family worship as springing from lukewarmness and worldliness in religion."[24]

The prince of preachers, Charles Spurgeon (1834-1892), spoke often about family worship. In one place he said,

If we want to bring up a godly family, who shall be a seed to serve God when our heads are under the clods of the valley, let us seek to train them up in the fear of God by meeting together as a family for worship.[25]

Spurgeon practiced what he preached. After his death, his wife Susannah wrote this glimpse into their lives together with their twin boys, both of whom became pastors:

---

[24] Alexander, 145.
[25] C. H. Spurgeon, "A Pastoral Visit," 362-363.

After the meal was over, an adjournment was made to the study for family worship, and it was at these seasons that my beloved's prayers were remarkable for their tender childlikeness, their spiritual pathos, and their intense devotion. He seemed to come as near to God as a little child to a loving father, and we were often moved to tears as he talked thus face to face with his Lord.[26]

A visitor to the Spurgeon home once wrote,

One of the most helpful hours of my visits to Westwood was the hour of family prayer. At six o'clock all the household gathered into the study for worship. Usually Mr. Spurgeon would himself lead the devotions. The portion read was invariably accompanied with exposition. How amazingly helpful those homely and gracious comments were. I remember, especially, his reading of the twenty-fourth of Luke: "Jesus Himself drew near and went with them." How sweetly he talked upon having Jesus with us wherever we go. Not only to have Him draw near at special seasons, but to go with us whatever labour we undertake. . . . Then, how full of tender pleading, of serene confidence in God, of world-embracing sympathy were his prayers,

[26] C. H. Spurgeon, *C. H. Spurgeon's Autobiography*. Susannah Spurgeon and J. W. Harrald (comps.). (London: Passmore and Alabaster, 1899; reprint, Pasadena, Tex.: Pilgrim Publications, 1992), 64.

. . . His public prayers were an inspiration and benediction, but his prayers with the family were to me more wonderful still. . . . Mr. Spurgeon, when bowed before God in family prayer, appeared a grander man even than when holding thousands spellbound by his oratory. [27]

John G. Paton (1824-1907) was a missionary to cannibals in the Hebrides islands of the South Pacific in the last half of the nineteenth century. Once when writing about his father, he noted how as a young man he appealed to his father (John's grandfather) to maintain family worship every day of the week and not just on Sunday. The result was that as a teenager, he himself often led the daily gathering of his parents and siblings in worship. "And so began," writes John Paton of his father,

in his seventeenth year that blessed custom of Family Prayer, morning and evening, which my father practiced probably without one single avoidable omission till he lay on his deathbed, seventy-seven years of age; when, even to the last day of his life, a portion of Scripture was read, and his voice was heard softly joining in the Psalm, and his lips breathed the morning and evening

---

[27] Arnold Dallimore. *Spurgeon: A New Biography* (Edinburgh: The Banner of Truth Trust, 1985), 178-179.

Prayer,—falling in sweet benediction on the heads of all his children, far away many of them over all the earth, but all meeting him there at the Throne of Grace. None of us can remember that any day ever passed unhallowed thus; no hurry for market, no rush to business, no arrival of friends or guests, no trouble or sorrow, no joy or excitement, ever prevented at least our kneeling around the family altar, while the High Priest led our prayers to God, and offered himself and his children there. And blessed to others, as well as to ourselves, was the light of such example! I have heard that in long after-years, the worst woman in the village of Torthorwald, then leading an immoral life, but since changed by the grace of God, was known to declare, that the only thing that kept her from despair and from the Hell of the suicide, was when in the dark winter nights she crept close up underneath my father's window, and heard him pleading in Family Worship that God would convert "the sinner from the error of wicked ways, and polish him as a jewel for the Redeemer's crown." "I felt," said she, "that I was a burden on that good man's heart, and I knew that God would not disappoint *him*. That thought kept me out of Hell, and at last led me to the only Saviour."[28]

---

[28] John G. Paton, *Missionary to the New Hebrides* (London: The Banner of Truth Trust, 1965), 14-15.

One of the most influential preachers of the twentieth century was Martyn Lloyd-Jones (1899-1981) of London. Iain Murray, his assistant pastor and later Lloyd-Jones' biographer, wrote that family worship was an essential part of his Christianity. "Family prayer marked the close of every day, and after his death Bethan Lloyd-Jones was to say that it was here that she experienced her greatest loss."[29]

In the twenty-first century, internationally-known pastor and author, John Piper (b. 1946), has emphasized the imperative of a man's fundamental commitment to family worship: "You have to decide how important you think these family moments are. It is possible for little ones and teenagers and parents. You may have to work at it. But it can be done."[30]

We could summarize the views of our Christian heroes across the centuries with a sentence from Jonathan Edwards: "Every Christian family ought to be as it were a little church."[31] And part of the life of that little church, of course, would include family worship.

---

[29] Iain Murray, *D. Martyn Lloyd-Jones, The Fight of Faith: 1939-1981* (Edinburgh: The Banner of Truth Trust, 1990), 763.

[30] John Piper, *Pierced by the Word* (Sisters, Ore.: Multnomah, 2003), 73.

[31] Edwards, *Works*, I:ccvi.

CHAPTER 3

"READ, PRAY, AND SING"

THE ELEMENTS OF FAMILY WORSHIP

Basically, there are three elements to family worship: read the Bible, pray, and sing. Only three syllables to remember—read, pray, sing. Jerry Marcellino, in his useful booklet, *Recovering the Lost Treasure of Family Worship*[32] uses three S's as a reminder: Scripture, supplication, and song. But the elements are so simple that you probably will not need any reminders about what to do.

- *Read the Bible.* Chapter-by-chapter, read through books of the Bible together. The younger the children, the more you will want to use narrative passages and shorter sections.[33] As the children get older, set a goal of a complete reading of the New Testament, and later of the entire Bible. Read enthusiastically and interpretively. Explain words the children may not understand. Clarify the meaning of key verses. To improve their understanding, ask the children to explain a particular verse or phrase to you.

---

[32] Jerry Marcellino, *Rediscovering the Lost Treasure of Family Worship* (Laurel, Miss.: Audubon Press, 1996).

[33] Since 1935, countless families have used Catherine Vos' *The Child's Story Bible* (Eerdmans) for reading the narrative passages of the Bible to children ages four to ten.

- *Pray.* Whether prayer is offered by the father only, or by one he designates, or by the entire family, be sure to pray together. Some people keep a prayer list. Some simply ask for prayer requests from the family. Whatever your approach, pray about at least one thing suggested by the passage you have read. Many families go to the book of Psalms and turn the words of a few verses there into a prayer. If praying through the twenty-third Psalm, for instance, after reading the first verse you might thank the Lord for being your Shepherd, asking Him to shepherd your family through certain events or decisions before you, and so forth. As you have time, continue through the passage line-by-line, speaking to God about what comes to mind while reading the text. By so doing you will not only pray for your family (in fresh and unique ways), but also teach them by example how to pray.

- *Sing.* Get hymnals for everyone. Your church may have some unused or older ones you could acquire. Your pastor or another worship leader at your church may be able to recommend other songbooks. The lyrics of many older, public domain (that is, not copyrighted) songs are available free on the Internet. Some people sing a different song each time; some sing the same song for a week so they can learn it. As to music, some families sing along with recordings, while others utilize family musicians, and many simply sing without accompaniment. Remember: with this and all other elements of family worship, some preparation is worthwhile, but not necessary. Just sit down and read, pray, and sing.

Spurgeon concurs, "I agree with Matthew Henry when he says, 'They that pray in the family do well; they that pray and read the Scriptures do better; but they that pray, and read, and sing do best of all.' There is a completeness in that kind of family worship which is much to be desired."[34]

On those occasions of family worship when time permits, consider these additions to the normal routine of "read, pray, sing":

- *Catechize.* Used for centuries by Christians in virtually all traditions, catechizing is a question-and-answer approach to teaching biblical doctrine. I have seen catechisms used successfully with children as young as two. For example, "Who made you?" is the

[34] C. H. Spurgeon, "The Happy Duty of Daily Praise," *Metropolitan Tabernacle Pulpit*, vol. 32 (London: Passmore and Alabaster, 1886; reprint, Pasadena, Tex.: Pilgrim Publications, 1986), 289.

first question asked in one catechism for very small children. Then the children are taught to answer, "God made me." The questions are reviewed and new ones are learned incrementally so that over time the children absorb a tremendous amount of biblical truth. A good, age-appropriate catechism is as valuable for learning the Bible as memorizing multiplication tables is for learning mathematics. Ask your pastor for recommendations, or search for catechisms on the Internet.

- *Memorize Scripture.* Family worship is a great time to review Scripture the family members have learned separately or collectively. Some families choose to work on one or more verses from the book of the Bible they are currently reading, others use different plans. Even learning just one verse per month is valuable and takes little time.

- *Read other books.* If time allows, you might begin your gathering together with some general family reading, after which you enter family worship. Or, at the close of family worship, you might take advantage of the opportunity to read a Christian book or biography to your family.

Beyond these content-related guidelines, consider these three reminders for your family's daily worship of God:

- *Brevity.* Be brief. Otherwise the experience can become tedious. It is always easy to lengthen the time if the occasion seems to be especially meaningful.

- *Regularity.* Try to have a regular time each day for family worship. For some people it works best early in the morning before the family scatters. For others, the most convenient time is at the close of the evening meal. If this is your choice, part of setting the table might include putting the Bible and songbooks close at hand. I would also recommend that you not allow anyone to get up from table until family worship is finished. For once someone says, "Just let me do this first," the others can become impatient or think of things they also need to do, and the sense of family togetherness is lost. A third popular time for family worship is late in the evening or at bedtime.

- *Flexibility.* Whatever time you choose, consider the wisdom of adapting a time when the family is already accustomed to being together, rather than trying to create another routine gathering during the day. Of course, a set time for family worship each day does not fit the schedule of many families. Every family has to flex its worship time sometime. Just make sure that your flexibility does not lead to inconsistency. Nevertheless, if developing an entirely new family routine is what it takes to begin family worship, the benefits will be worth whatever it costs.

CHAPTER 4

"NO FAMILY WORSHIP SITUATION IS UNIQUE"

BUT WHAT IF . . . ?

Several specific situations commonly prompt questions about the feasibility of family worship.

1. *What if the father is not a Christian?*

The Bible gives no instruction in this case, and Christian moms have responded to this situation in various ways. Many have discovered that their unbelieving husbands are quite willing to read the Bible with their families—they only had to be asked. An appeal by the wife, especially when the children join in, with an emphasis on how this will improve family togetherness is sometimes all it takes. Even unbelieving men are often quite aware of the need for the family to spend more time together, but are unsure of how to make it happen. If the rest of the family comes up with a solution to a need he himself feels, he may gladly go along. He may have questions about what to do or doubts about whether he can do it, but the wife can deal with these issues in her appeal, explaining that she and the children can help with the praying and singing.

Of course, there are many unbelieving husbands who will not participate in family worship under any circumstances.

In that case, the mom should institute and lead family worship herself, being careful that the practice of family worship or her spirit about it does not cause unnecessary offense or turn the children against their father.

2. *What if there is no father at home?*

The responsibility in this case falls to the mother to bring up the children "in the discipline and instruction of the Lord" (Ephesians 6:4), and this includes family worship. If she has a son, she might allow him to have an increasing role in family worship, just as John Paton's father often led family worship when he was a teenager. She might ask some of the leaders of the church to come by on a regular basis and conduct family worship while there. If you are a woman in this situation, ask the Lord to make you a grandmother like Lois or a mother like Eunice, women who were credited by the apostle Paul in 2 Timothy 1:5 with transmitting their faith to Timothy.

3. *What if the children are very young?*

You exercise discipline and patience, and proceed with family worship. Part of the discipline may be to teach them to stay in a certain place—such as by their mother, or on a particular rug—and to be quiet during the few moments of family worship. Part of the patience is persevering with the practice of family worship even though the children want to play and not pay attention. Young children cannot concentrate or understand at the same level as older children, so families whose children are all quite small should aim for only a very short time of family worship. As much as possible, accommodate what you read and what you sing to their ages. At the very least, in these fast growing years you will begin to make lasting impressions upon them about the habit and the value of family worship in your home.

4. *What if there is a wide range of ages among the children?*

This is often the case, and has as many advantages as it has challenges. In reality, this difficulty involves only one part of family worship—the time in the Scriptures—for all the family can sing and pray. When you read the Bible together, you will have to make a point to explain and apply things at different levels. You can ask questions suitable to the age of each child. The younger ones may pick up more than you realize when you are teaching the older ones. The older ones can learn from your example how to teach younger ones so they can do the same in their own families some day. Regardless of the challenges to the practice of family worship that exist in large families, it can be done, for throughout the history of the church, families have typically been larger and more diverse in ages than is common today, and yet they were often more faithful in family worship than Christians are now.

Just remember that there is no family worship situation that has not been addressed by Christians for centuries. You are not alone in the circumstances that make family worship difficult. We tend to think that we have unique problems, and our flesh wants to excuse us from family worship on the false grounds that our situation is an exception. We need to accept the fact that in this sinful world, challenges to family worship arise regularly in every home.

Nevertheless, we must stand on this bedrock truth: God deserves to be worshiped daily in our homes by our families. And for that reason, *start today.*

CHAPTER 5

"ISN'T THIS WHAT YOU REALLY *WANT* TO DO?"

START TODAY

The worthiness of God to receive your family's worship each day is reason enough to start practicing family worship today. But in addition to that, consider these good motivations:

- What better way to evangelize your children daily?
- What better way to provide a regular time for your children to learn the things of God from you?
- What better way to provide your children with an ongoing opportunity to ask about the things of God in a comfortable context for such questions?
- What better way for you to transmit your core beliefs to your children?
- What better way for your children to see the ongoing spiritual example of their parents?
- What better way to provide workable, reproducible examples to your children of how to have a distinctively Christian home when they start a home of their own?
- What better way for getting your family together on a daily basis?
- Isn't this what you really *want* to do?

Despite the desire that many men have to begin family worship, some simply lack the resolve. In his *Thoughts on Family Worship*, J. W. Alexander answers eight common objections to starting family worship, but then says that a "single reason operates with more force than all the others put together." It is when a man says—most likely only to himself—"The truth is, I am ashamed to begin."[35]

This is when a man awakens to his responsibility, but because he has failed to lead family worship for so long he feels embarrassed to begin now. Or he fears the sneer of some member of his family when he says he wants to begin daily family worship. Or he is afraid that he is not capable of leading in family worship. Or he is ashamed because, even though he has tried something like this before, he did not stick with it.

For some men it may be nothing more than the embarrassment of not knowing what to say to their wives and children to get family worship started. Men, all you have to say is something like this: "I have come to believe that the Bible teaches I should be leading us in family worship, and I want to start today. I have a lot to learn about it, but I want to do what is right. Will you join me?"

Husbands, fathers—have the resolve of Jacob in Genesis 35:2-3:

---

[35] Alexander, 151.

So Jacob said to his household and to all who were with him, 'Put away the foreign gods which are among you, and purify yourselves and change your garments; and let us arise and go up to Bethel, and I will make an altar there to God, who answered me in the day of my distress and has been with me wherever I have gone.

Like Jacob, have the manly resolve to tell your family that you want to make an altar to God in your home; that is, you want to make your home a place of worship to God. Exhort the family to put away anything that would keep them from worshiping God with you, and to arise and follow you as you lead them in worshiping God.

Let me tell you about a man who had the resolve of Jacob. We are back to the story of missionary John G. Paton and his father, under whose window the immoral woman would come to listen to their family worship. This is the scene of Paton leaving home for the last time, going to the school from which he would then leave for the mission field.

My dear father walked with me the first six miles of the way. His counsels and tears and heavenly conversation on that parting journey are fresh in my heart as if it had been but yesterday; and tears are on my cheeks as freely now as then, whenever memory steals me away to the scene. For the last half-mile or so we walked on together in almost unbroken silence,—my father, as was often his custom, carrying hat in hand, while his long, flowing yellow hair (then yellow, but in later years white as snow) streamed like a girl's down his shoulders. His lips kept moving in silent prayers for me; and his tears fell fast when our eyes met each other in looks for which all speech was vain! We halted on reaching the appointed parting place; he grasped my hand firmly for a minute in silence, and then solemnly and affectionately said:

"God bless you, my son! Your father's God prosper you, and keep you from evil!"

Unable to say more, his lips kept moving in silent prayer; in tears we embraced, and parted. I ran off as fast as I could; and, when about to turn a corner in the road where he would lose sight of me, I looked back and saw him still standing with head uncovered where I had left him—gazing after me. Waving my hat in adieu, I was round the corner and out of sight in an instant. But my heart was too full and sore to carry me further, so I darted into the side of the road and wept for a time. Then, rising up cautiously, I climbed the dyke to see if he yet stood where I had left him; and just at that moment I caught a glimpse of him climbing the dyke and looking out for me! He did not see me, and after he had gazed eagerly in my direction for a while he got down, set his face towards home, and began to return—his head still uncovered, and his heart, I felt sure, still rising in prayers for me. I watched through blinding tears, till his form faded from my gaze; and then, hastening on my way, vowed deeply and oft, by the help of God, to live and act so as never to grieve or dishonour such a father and mother as He had given me. The appearance of my father, when we parted—his advice, prayers, and tears—the road, the dyke, the climbing up on it and then walking away, head uncovered—have often, often, all through life, risen vividly before my mind, and do so now while I am writing, as if it had been but an hour ago. In my earlier years particularly, when exposed to many temptations, his parting form rose before me as that of a guardian Angel. It is no Pharisaism, but deep gratitude, which makes me here testify that the memory of that scene not only helped, by God's grace, to keep me pure from the prevailing sins, but also stimulated me in all my studies, that I might not fall short of his hopes, and in all my Christian duties, that I might faithfully follow his shining example.[36]

What had led Paton to such a love of his father and his father's example? Paton answers,

---

[36] Paton, 25-26.

How much my father's prayers at this time impressed me I can never explain, nor could any stranger understand. When, on his knees and all of us kneeling around him in Family Worship, he poured out his whole soul with tears for the conversion of the Heathen World to the service of Jesus, and for every personal and domestic need, we all felt as if in the presence of the living Saviour, and learned to know and love Him as our Divine Friend. As we rose from our knees, I used to look at the light on my father's face, and wish I were like him in spirit,—hoping that, in answer to his prayers, I might be privileged and prepared to carry the blessed Gospel to some portion of the Heathen World.[37]

I will tell you about another man who had the resolve of Jacob. Rick Husband was commander of the Space Shuttle *Columbia*, and among the seven astronauts killed February 1, 2003, when the spacecraft broke apart and disintegrated over Texas just sixteen minutes from their landing in Florida. The day after the tragedy, a memorial service was held for the forty-five-year-old Husband and fellow astronaut Mike Anderson at Grace Community Church in Houston where they attended. At that service, a video was played where Husband said,

---

[37] Paton, 21.

If I ended up at the end of my life having been an astronaut, but having sacrificed my family along the way or living my life in a way that didn't glorify God, then I would look back on it with great regret. Having become an astronaut would not really have mattered all that much. And I finally came to realize that what really meant the most to me was to try and live my life the way God wanted me to and to try and be a good husband to Evelyn and to be a good father to my children.[38]

But there is more to Rick Husband's resolve to be a good husband and father than mere words. A week prior to leaving for the flight crew's quarantine, Commander Husband turned to his wife, Evelyn, and said, "I want to make a videotape for Laura and one for Matthew that they can watch each day I'm in orbit. I want the children to know how much I love them and that I'll be thinking about them every day."[39]

At the beginning of the tape he left with his seven-year-old son, Husband said,

Hi, Matthew. I wanted to tell you how much I love you

---

[38] "Rick Husband, Mike Anderson 'fervently lived for God,'" Baptist Press, February 3, 2003.

[39] Evelyn Husband with Donna VanLiere, *High Calling* (Nashville: Thomas Nelson, 2003) 2.

and I wanted to make this tape for you so that you and I could have a devotional time for every day that I'm in space. So, what I am doing is I'm looking at your devotional book and I'm starting on the sixteenth of January, which is our launch day, and what I will do is read through this book and read the Bible verse also and go through the whole thing just like you and I are sitting here on the couch together. I just wanted to do this because I love you so much and I'm going to do one for your sister as well.[40]

How precious do you think those eighteen devotions on video are to that family today? Isn't this the kind of legacy you want to leave to your family? Isn't family worship what you really *want* to do?

Fathers, husbands—if you have been negligent in this duty and great privilege, repent by starting family worship today. Again, you may feel awkward about what to say to your wife or your children about starting, but simply say that God has convicted you of your responsibility to lead in family worship and you want to start at a given time today or tonight. Almost certainly your wife will be thrilled more than you can imagine to hear you say that. Your children may or may not be as enthusiastic, but that does not really matter. The less interested they are, the more your family needs family worship.

---

[40] Husband, 222.

The Lord will help you. He does not call His Spirit-begotten sons to this task without giving them the power of the Holy Spirit to accomplish it. The same Father who gave you the Gospel and who drew you to Christ will strengthen you by His Spirit to put on this badge of godly manhood.

Family members—have the willing spirit of Jacob's household. After he called them to follow his leadership in the family worship of God, Genesis 35:4 tells us, "So they gave to Jacob all the foreign gods which they had and the rings which were in their ears, and Jacob hid them under the oak which was near Shechem." Respond just as willingly to the call to family worship in your home. Encourage your husband or dad in his desire to bring the blessing of God upon you. Do not be a stumbling block in his efforts to obey God.

Single men—resolve to begin a time of worship with your fiancé from the night you become engaged. Build your marriage from the start on the foundation of family worship. This is holy husbanding. And it is much easier to begin the worship of God together before your wedding day than after your habits and routines of married life have become established.

Single women—resolve not to marry a man who will not pray with you daily and lead you in family worship. For if he will not lead you in this way before you are married, it is very unlikely that he will do so after you are married. If a man shows an interest in marrying you, talk to him about family worship before you commit your life and the lives of your future children to him.

Let us be clear: faithful involvement in family worship is not the Gospel. We are not made right with God by practicing family worship, or by the way we love our families, or by anything else we do. The Gospel—the message that can lead to being right with God—is the truth of what God has done through the life, death, resurrection, and ascension of Jesus Christ. The most important way to respond to that message is not engagement in family worship, but first to repent of your sins against God and to believe that Jesus can make you right with God. But blessed is the family where the good news of what God has done through Jesus Christ is declared and discussed, day after day, generation after generation.

Regardless of what anyone else does, let every father, let every Christian commit himself to this: "As for me and my house, we will serve the Lord" in family worship.

Discussion Guide

Chapter 1

"As for me and my house, we will serve the Lord."
Family Worship in the Bible

1. What did you learn in this chapter about the role of family worship in Old Testament times?
2. Which Old Testament passages make the strongest argument for the necessity of family worship?
3. What New Testament texts do you consider most important regarding the necessity of family worship?
4. Can you think of other biblical texts or doctrines which relate to family worship?
5. What are the key Scripture passages which indicate that the responsibility for initiating and conducting family worship lies on the shoulders of the husband/father?
6. Why does the Bible place the responsibility for leading family worship on the husband/father?

"HERE THE REFORMATION MUST BEGIN"

FAMILY WORSHIP IN CHURCH HISTORY

1. What impressed you most about the practice of family worship among some of the heroes of church history?

2. Why does the Westminster *Directory for Family Worship* call for church discipline for those men who fail to lead their families in worship?

3. Why would Matthew Henry say of family worship, "Here the reformation must begin"?

4. In the opinion of the author, what is one of the best books ever written on the subject of family worship, and how may families profit from reading it?

5. What are some of the beliefs about family worship that all these Christian heroes apparently held in common?

6. In what ways do you think the practice of family worship was easier in previous centuries than today? Harder? The same?

Chapter 3

"Read, Pray, and Sing"

The Elements of Family Worship

1. What are the three primary elements of family worship?

2. What suggestions have you found effective for reading the Bible with children?

3. What are some practices to avoid when reading the Bible with children?

4. In addition to the ones found in chapter three, what are other workable ideas for praying in family worship?

5. In addition to the ones found in chapter three, what are other workable ideas for singing in family worship?

6. What are some optional elements that families may incorporate into their worship?

7. What does catechizing in family worship look like?

8. What are some of the benefits of catechizing in family worship?

9. What are some practical tips for families wanting to memorize Scripture together in family worship?

10. What books come to mind as supplemental reading in family worship?

11. On average, how much time would be appropriate for each of the three primary elements of family worship?

12. Why is it important to have a regular time each day for family worship?

13. Why do we need to be both encouraged toward and cautioned against flexibility in the time and duration of family worship?

Chapter 4

"No family worship situation is unique"
But What If . . . ?

1. What are the most important observations to keep in mind in these family worship situations:
    a. If the father is not a Christian?
    b. If there is no father at home?
    c. If the children are very young?
    d. If there is a wide range of ages among the children?

2. What other common difficulties with family worship should be discussed?

3. Since so many possible family worship difficulties exist, why are none of them unique?

CHAPTER 5

"ISN'T THIS WHAT YOU REALLY *WANT* TO DO?"

START TODAY

1. What are some of the practical benefits of family worship?

2. What kinds of things might a man say to his wife and family when he wants to begin the practice of family worship? What kinds of things should *not* be said?

3. What kinds of things might a wife and/or children say to appeal to their husband/father to begin the practice of family worship? What kinds of things should *not* be said?

4. How can the local church help families begin and continue family worship?

5. Why is it important for single adults to make commitments to family worship before they commit themselves to someone in marriage?

6. What is one thing you believe God would have you do now in regard to family worship?

Author

Donald S. Whitney has been Associate Professor of Biblical Spirituality and Director of Applied Ministry at The Southern Baptist Theological Seminary in Louisville, Kentucky, since 2005. Before that he held a similar position at Midwestern Baptist Theological Seminary in Kansas City, Missouri, for ten years. He is the founder and president of The Center for Biblical Spirituality.

Don grew up in Osceola, Arkansas, where he came to believe in Jesus Christ as Lord and Savior. He was active in sports throughout high school and college, and worked in the radio station his dad managed. After graduating from Arkansas State University, Don planned to finish law school and pursue a career in sportscasting. While at the University of Arkansas School of Law, he sensed God's call to preach the Gospel of Jesus Christ. He then enrolled at Southwestern Baptist Theological Seminary in Fort Worth, Texas, graduating with a Master of Divinity degree in 1979. In 1987, Don earned a Doctor of Ministry degree at Trinity Evangelical Divinity School in Deerfield, Illinois. Currently, he is completing his Doctor of Theology with Specialization in Christian Spirituality at the University of South Africa.

Prior to his ministry as a seminary professor, Don was pastor of Glenfield Baptist Church in Glen Ellyn, Illinois (a Chicago suburb) for almost fifteen years. Altogether, he has served local churches in pastoral ministry for twenty-four years.

He is the author of *Spiritual Disciplines for the Christian Life* (NavPress, 1991), which has a companion discussion guide. He has also written *How Can I Be Sure I'm A Christian* (NavPress, 1994), *Spiritual Disciplines Within the Church* (Moody Press, 1996), *Ten Questions to Diagnose Your Spiritual Health* (NavPress, 2001), and *Simplify Your Spiritual Life* (NavPress, 2003).

Don's wife, Caffy, ministers from their home in the Louisville area as a women's Bible study teacher, an artist, and a freelance illustrator. Her website is www.CaffyWhitney.com. The Whitneys are parents of a daughter, Laurelen Christiana.

Information about Don's books (including sample chapters), downloadable bulletin inserts, his speaking schedule, subscription information for Don's free, email newsletter, and other materials from The Center for Biblical Spirituality are all available at his website, **www.BiblicalSpirituality.org**.